PRINCEWILL LAGANG

Cherish and Honor: Christian Marriage Values

First published by PRINCEWILL LAGANG 2023

Copyright © 2023 by Princewill Lagang

All rights reserved. No part of this publication may be reproduced, stored or transmitted in any form or by any means, electronic, mechanical, photocopying, recording, scanning, or otherwise without written permission from the publisher. It is illegal to copy this book, post it to a website, or distribute it by any other means without permission.

Princewill Lagang asserts the moral right to be identified as the author of this work.

First edition

This book was professionally typeset on Reedsy.
Find out more at reedsy.com

# Contents

| | | |
|---|---|---|
| 1 | Cherish and Honor: Christian Marriage Values | 1 |
| 2 | The Foundation of Faith | 4 |
| 3 | Love that Cherishes | 7 |
| 4 | Honor and Respect | 10 |
| 5 | The Power of Forgiveness | 13 |
| 6 | A Journey Together | 16 |
| 7 | Cherish and Honor for a Lifetime | 19 |
| 8 | The Continuation of Tradition | 21 |
| 9 | Cherish and Honor in the Modern World | 24 |
| 10 | A Testament of Faith | 27 |
| 11 | Nurturing Love for Generations | 30 |
| 12 | A Love That Endures | 33 |

# 1

# Cherish and Honor: Christian Marriage Values

The soft, golden hues of the setting sun bathed the quaint, whitewashed church in a warm glow. As the doors creaked open, Sarah's heart raced. She clutched her father's arm as they began the slow, solemn march down the aisle. Her eyes locked onto John, waiting at the altar, his face a mix of nervousness and eager anticipation. Today, they would commit to a lifetime together, guided by the timeless values of Christian marriage.

This chapter, titled "Cherish and Honor: Christian Marriage Values," embarks on a journey into the heart of Christian matrimony, where love and faith intertwine to form a bond that transcends the earthly realm.

1.1 The Sacred Covenant

Christian marriage is rooted in the belief that it is not just a legal or social contract but a sacred covenant before God. It is a commitment to love, cherish, and honor one another, mirroring the love Christ has for His Church. In Ephesians 5:25, the Apostle Paul writes, "Husbands, love your wives, just as Christ loved the Church and gave himself up for her." This verse sets the tone for the high standards of love and selflessness expected in Christian marriages.

## 1.2 A Foundation of Faith

For Sarah and John, as for many other Christian couples, faith plays a pivotal role in their relationship. It is the bedrock upon which they build their lives together. Their faith provides them with strength, guidance, and a moral compass in their journey through the complexities of married life.

## 1.3 Love that Cherishes

The word 'cherish' is woven into the fabric of Christian marriage. It signifies a love that goes beyond mere affection, one that cares for, protects, and holds in the highest regard. To cherish a spouse is to understand the profound value they hold as a gift from God. In 1 Corinthians 13:4-7, love is described as patient, kind, not envious or boastful, not proud or self-seeking. This profound love, guided by faith, forms the cornerstone of a Christian marriage.

## 1.4 Honor and Respect

Honor in a Christian marriage is not merely about showing respect; it's about recognizing the unique worth of each spouse. It's about uplifting one another and honoring the divine image in which they are created. 1 Peter 3:7 says, "Husbands, in the same way be considerate as you live with your wives, and treat them with respect." This principle of mutual respect and honor is a powerful force that fosters harmony and unity.

## 1.5 The Power of Forgiveness

As in all relationships, Christian marriages are not immune to challenges and conflicts. But forgiveness, another Christian virtue, plays a crucial role in healing wounds and restoring harmony. In Matthew 6:14-15, Jesus teaches,

"For if you forgive other people when they sin against you, your heavenly Father will also forgive you." The ability to forgive is a reflection of the forgiveness received from God.

## 1.6 A Journey Together

Sarah and John's wedding day is not the culmination of their love story, but the beginning of a lifelong journey. As they embark on this voyage guided by Christian values, they know that their love will deepen, their faith will strengthen, and their commitment to cherish and honor one another will stand as a testament to their love and fidelity.

In this chapter, we will explore these foundational Christian marriage values in greater detail, delving into the biblical teachings, real-life examples, and practical advice for couples seeking to build a marriage that not only survives but thrives, anchored in the enduring principles of Christian faith.

# 2

# The Foundation of Faith

In the serene chapel where Sarah and John exchanged their vows, faith was not just a backdrop; it was the very foundation upon which their marriage stood. This chapter, titled "The Foundation of Faith," takes a closer look at how faith in a Christian marriage shapes the relationship, provides strength, and adds a spiritual dimension to the union.

2.1 Faith as the Cornerstone

For Sarah and John, and countless other Christian couples, faith is not an abstract concept; it's the cornerstone of their lives together. Faith in God and faith in each other intertwine to create a bond that is both strong and resilient. This chapter explores the role of faith as a foundation and the source of strength in their marriage.

2.2 Prayer as a Connection

Prayer is a powerful tool in a Christian marriage. It is a way for couples to connect not only with God but also with each other on a deeper level. It provides a space to share joys, worries, and hopes, and to seek guidance in moments of uncertainty. The act of praying together strengthens the spiritual connection between spouses.

## 2.3 Trust in Divine Guidance

Many Christian couples rely on their faith to guide them in important decisions, both big and small. Trusting in divine guidance offers a sense of reassurance, as they believe God is an active participant in their journey. This faith-based decision-making process can lead to a more profound unity between spouses.

## 2.4 Navigating Challenges Through Faith

No marriage is without its challenges, and Christian marriages are no exception. However, faith equips couples with the resilience to face difficulties with grace and hope. It is a source of comfort in times of sorrow, a motivator in times of doubt, and a source of inspiration for overcoming obstacles.

## 2.5 A Source of Moral Compass

Christian marriages are guided by a moral compass deeply rooted in the teachings of Christ. The Bible offers a clear framework for ethical behavior and how to treat one another. This chapter delves into how Christian values influence decision-making and moral choices within a marriage.

## 2.6 The Spiritual Bond

In Christian marriages, the bond between spouses extends beyond the physical and emotional realms into the spiritual. As Ephesians 5:31-32 describes, "For this reason a man will leave his father and mother and be united to his wife, and the two will become one flesh." This spiritual unity is strengthened by faith, making the couple's journey truly transformative.

As we explore the various dimensions of faith within Christian marriages, this chapter provides insights into how couples like Sarah and John navigate life's challenges, cherish and honor one another, and deepen their commitment to a love grounded in faith. It sheds light on the enduring role of faith as the cornerstone of a Christian marriage, offering both strength and spiritual fulfillment as the journey unfolds.

# 3

# Love that Cherishes

Love is at the heart of every marriage, but in a Christian marriage, it is love that cherishes – a love that transcends the ordinary and embraces the divine. In this chapter, "Love that Cherishes," we delve into the profound depths of this unique Christian concept and how it shapes the dynamics of a marriage.

3.1 Beyond Ordinary Love

Christian love is not simply a romantic sentiment or an emotional attachment; it is a love that mirrors the love Christ has for His Church. It is a sacrificial, enduring, and selfless love, characterized by its ability to cherish and nurture the beloved. This chapter explores the rich meaning of love within the Christian context.

3.2 The Biblical Basis of Cherishing Love

The Bible provides a wealth of guidance on how love should be expressed within a Christian marriage. Passages such as 1 Corinthians 13, often referred to as the "love chapter," outline the attributes of love – patience, kindness, humility, selflessness, and forgiveness. These biblical teachings form the blueprint for cherishing love.

## 3.3 The Role of Sacrifice

A central aspect of cherishing love is the willingness to sacrifice for one's spouse. This act of selflessness reflects Christ's sacrifice for His Church. In John 15:13, Jesus says, "Greater love has no one than this: to lay down one's life for one's friends." In a Christian marriage, spouses are called to make similar sacrificial gestures, whether in big or small ways.

## 3.4 Nurturing and Protecting

Cherishing love is also about nurturing and protecting one another. It involves fostering emotional, spiritual, and physical well-being within the marriage. This chapter explores how couples can create an environment that allows love to flourish and spouses to thrive.

## 3.5 The Power of Commitment

The commitment to cherish one another is a lifelong vow. It means choosing to love, honor, and cherish one's spouse every day, even when the initial sparks of romance have faded. This enduring commitment reflects the constancy of God's love and serves as an anchor in the storms of life.

## 3.6 A Legacy of Cherishing Love

Through the stories of Christian couples who have weathered the tests of time, this chapter offers real-life examples of cherishing love in action. It demonstrates how love can deepen and grow, leaving a legacy for future generations to follow.

As we journey through this chapter, we will explore the facets of cherishing love in Christian marriages. From the biblical foundations to the practical applications, we will uncover the profound beauty of love that cherishes, and how it enriches the lives of those who seek to honor and cherish each other in the sacred covenant of Christian marriage.

# 4

# Honor and Respect

In the sacred institution of Christian marriage, honor and respect are not optional virtues; they are the cornerstone upon which the relationship stands. In this chapter, "Honor and Respect," we explore the deep significance of these values within Christian matrimony and how they contribute to the health and longevity of a marriage.

4.1 The Importance of Honor

Honor is an acknowledgment of the intrinsic worth of one's spouse. In 1 Peter 2:17, the Bible instructs believers to "Honor everyone. Love the brotherhood. Fear God. Honor the emperor." This concept extends to honoring one's spouse as an act of reverence for the divine image within them.

4.2 Respect as a Form of Love

Respect is a tangible expression of love in a Christian marriage. It means recognizing the dignity of one's spouse, treating them with courtesy, and valuing their opinions, feelings, and perspectives. When respect is present, love thrives.

4.3 Mutual Submission

Ephesians 5:21 reminds us of the importance of mutual submission in Christian marriage: "Submit to one another out of reverence for Christ." This submission is not about dominance or control but rather about a humble attitude that values the desires and needs of one's spouse.

4.4 Communication and Conflict Resolution

Honor and respect play a pivotal role in communication and conflict resolution within a Christian marriage. The way spouses communicate reflects their respect for one another. Healthy communication is grounded in active listening, empathy, and mutual respect. This chapter explores practical ways to improve communication and resolve conflicts while preserving honor and respect.

4.5 The Impact on Children and Families

Honor and respect within a Christian marriage create a positive atmosphere for children and extended family members. Children learn the values of honor and respect by observing their parents, and these values become a part of the family's legacy.

4.6 Honor and Respect in Action

This chapter will feature stories of Christian couples who exemplify honor and respect in their marriages. These real-life examples demonstrate the transformative power of these values in building strong, enduring relationships.

As we navigate through the pages of this chapter, we will uncover the multifaceted nature of honor and respect within Christian marriages. We will explore how these values affect communication, conflict resolution, and the overall health of the relationship. By witnessing the impact of honor and respect in the lives of Christian couples, we can better appreciate the essential role they play in building enduring, loving marriages.

# 5

# The Power of Forgiveness

Forgiveness is a cornerstone of Christian values, and within the context of marriage, it holds a special significance. In this chapter, "The Power of Forgiveness," we delve into the profound role that forgiveness plays in Christian matrimony and how it fosters healing, reconciliation, and the longevity of a marriage.

5.1 The Biblical Foundation of Forgiveness

The Bible is replete with teachings on forgiveness. In Ephesians 4:32, it is written, "Be kind and compassionate to one another, forgiving each other, just as in Christ God forgave you." This verse serves as a guiding principle for Christian couples, emphasizing the importance of forgiving one another as an act of obedience to God's example.

5.2 Forgiveness as an Act of Love

Forgiveness is a manifestation of love. It demonstrates the willingness to release grudges, resentments, and hurts for the sake of preserving the relationship. The act of forgiving acknowledges the imperfections of both partners and allows love to triumph over transgressions.

## 5.3 Healing Wounds and Restoring Trust

In a marriage, forgiveness serves as a balm for wounds and a path to restoring trust. It is a way for couples to mend the breaches that inevitably occur over time. This chapter explores the process of forgiveness and how it contributes to the healing of emotional and relational scars.

## 5.4 Embracing Humility

Forgiveness requires humility. It necessitates the acknowledgment of one's own shortcomings and a readiness to extend grace to one's spouse. The humility of forgiveness paves the way for reconciliation and growth within the marriage.

## 5.5 The Transformative Power of Forgiveness

Stories of real Christian couples who have overcome significant challenges through the power of forgiveness will be featured in this chapter. Their experiences highlight the transformative nature of forgiveness and how it can lead to stronger, more resilient marriages.

## 5.6 Forgiveness and Self-Forgiveness

This chapter also delves into the idea of self-forgiveness, as harboring guilt and self-condemnation can hinder a marriage's growth. Christian couples learn to forgive not only each other but also themselves, recognizing that they are fallible human beings in need of divine grace.

## 5.7 A Continual Practice

The practice of forgiveness is not a one-time event but a continual process in a Christian marriage. It requires patience, endurance, and a commitment to walking the path of love and reconciliation. This chapter provides practical advice on how couples can make forgiveness a natural part of their relationship.

By the end of this chapter, readers will gain a deep understanding of the significance of forgiveness in Christian marriage. They will witness how forgiveness can heal wounds, restore trust, and transform relationships. Moreover, they will see that forgiveness is not a sign of weakness but a powerful demonstration of Christian love and grace, enriching the sacred covenant of marriage.

# 6

# A Journey Together

As Sarah and John embarked on their journey of Christian marriage, they knew that their path would be both challenging and beautiful. This chapter, "A Journey Together," explores the dynamic and evolving nature of Christian marriages and the ways in which they grow, deepen, and adapt over time.

6.1 The Ongoing Adventure

Christian marriage is not a destination; it's a continual adventure. It is a journey that unfolds, offering new experiences, challenges, and opportunities for growth. This chapter delves into the idea that a Christian marriage is an ongoing process of discovery and development.

6.2 Growing Together in Faith

As a couple's journey progresses, so does their faith. Christian marriages provide the space for spouses to deepen their faith together. They learn, explore, and grow spiritually, finding new ways to connect with God and each other.

6.3 Overcoming Challenges

Every marriage faces trials and tribulations, and Christian marriages are no exception. The difference lies in the way couples approach these challenges. This chapter explores how faith and Christian values empower couples to overcome obstacles and emerge stronger.

6.4 Nurturing the Flame of Love

Love in a Christian marriage isn't static; it's dynamic. It evolves and deepens as the journey continues. This chapter examines the ways in which couples can nurture and rekindle their love, keeping the flame burning brightly.

6.5 A Supportive Community

Christian marriages are often embedded within a broader faith community that provides support, guidance, and encouragement. The chapter explores how these communities contribute to the strength and longevity of Christian marriages.

6.6 Leaving a Legacy

As a Christian marriage matures, it leaves a legacy not only for the couple's children but also for their extended families and friends. This legacy is a testament to the enduring power of faith, love, and commitment.

6.7 Celebrating Milestones

Christian marriages are marked by significant milestones, from anniversaries to the spiritual growth of children. This chapter provides insights on how to celebrate these moments and use them as opportunities for reflection and gratitude.

As we navigate through the pages of this chapter, we will gain a deeper understanding of the journey that is a Christian marriage. We will explore how faith, love, and Christian values continue to evolve and strengthen the bond between spouses. Whether in times of joy or adversity, Christian marriages are a testament to the enduring power of a shared faith and commitment, offering hope, inspiration, and a profound sense of purpose to those who embark on this sacred journey.

# 7

# Cherish and Honor for a Lifetime

In this final chapter, "Cherish and Honor for a Lifetime," we explore the lasting impact of Christian marriage values on the relationship of Sarah and John, their family, and the broader community. This chapter serves as a reflection on the enduring legacy of their love, faith, and commitment.

7.1 Embracing the Fullness of Time

As Sarah and John look back on their journey, they see how their love, faith, and values have evolved over time. They realize that their commitment to cherish and honor each other has deepened, and their love has grown richer as they've faced life's challenges together.

7.2 Passing on the Torch

The couple recognizes their role in passing on the torch of faith and values to the next generation. They have witnessed how their own commitment has influenced their children's understanding of love, honor, and faith. This chapter explores the profound responsibility and joy of instilling these values in their family.

7.3 Cherishing Traditions and Rituals

Sarah and John have established traditions and rituals in their marriage that reflect their Christian values. These customs serve as reminders of their commitment and bring continuity to their journey. This chapter explores the significance of such traditions and how they contribute to a lasting bond.

7.4 Strengthening the Community

Their commitment to cherish and honor each other has not only impacted their family but also their broader faith community. Their marriage serves as an example and source of inspiration for others, highlighting the transformative power of Christian values within the context of marriage.

7.5 The Golden Years

As the couple enters their golden years, their love endures, and their faith continues to sustain them. This chapter reflects on the joy of growing old together in a loving, Christian marriage, and the wisdom they've gained through the years.

7.6 Cherishing and Honoring Forever

As Sarah and John's journey continues, they remain dedicated to cherishing and honoring each other for a lifetime. Their commitment to these Christian marriage values is a testament to the enduring power of love, faith, and a shared devotion to God.

In this final chapter, we witness the lifelong impact of Christian marriage values as they manifest in the lives of Sarah and John. Their journey serves as an inspiration, a testimony to the lasting significance of cherishing and honoring one another within the sacred covenant of Christian marriage. This chapter closes their story while leaving readers with a profound understanding of the transformative power of these enduring values in the context of marriage.

# 8

# The Continuation of Tradition

In this concluding chapter, "The Continuation of Tradition," we delve into the broader impact of Christian marriage values on society and the role that traditions play in preserving and passing on these cherished values to future generations.

8.1 Cherish and Honor as Pillars of Society

The values of cherishing and honoring are not limited to the confines of individual marriages; they are fundamental pillars of a healthy society. This chapter explores how strong, faith-based marriages contribute to the well-being of communities and the world at large.

8.2 The Influence of Strong Marriages

Strong Christian marriages have a ripple effect on society. They provide stable environments for children to grow and develop, foster a culture of respect and love, and contribute to the overall welfare of communities. This chapter delves into the profound influence that healthy marriages have on society.

8.3 Preserving Values Through Tradition

Traditions play a pivotal role in preserving and passing on Christian marriage values. Families and communities develop customs and rituals that reflect the enduring values of cherishing and honoring. These traditions help reinforce the importance of these values in the lives of individuals.

8.4 Building a Legacy of Love

The legacy of love cultivated within Christian marriages becomes part of the wider cultural heritage. This chapter explores how the stories and examples of strong, faith-driven marriages inspire others to seek the same enduring love and commitment.

8.5 Nurturing Future Generations

Christian marriage values, when passed down through tradition, guide the moral and ethical development of future generations. Parents, grandparents, and communities share the responsibility of instilling these values in their children, teaching them how to cherish and honor one another.

8.6 Embracing Diversity

This chapter also highlights the inclusive nature of cherishing and honoring in Christian values. These principles can be applied to a diverse range of relationships and marriages, emphasizing love, respect, and faith as universal, unifying forces.

8.7 A Call to Action

The chapter concludes with a call to action, encouraging readers to reflect on their own relationships and the role of tradition in preserving Christian marriage values. It invites individuals to embrace these values, whether within the context of marriage or in their interactions with others.

As we journey through the final chapter, we contemplate the broader societal impact of Christian marriage values and the importance of traditions in passing on these values to future generations. The enduring legacy of cherishing and honoring is a testament to the transformative power of faith, love, and commitment, not only in individual lives but also in the culture and traditions that shape our world.

# 9

# Cherish and Honor in the Modern World

In this chapter, "Cherish and Honor in the Modern World," we explore the ways in which Christian marriage values of cherishing and honoring have evolved to meet the challenges and opportunities of contemporary society. It examines how these values remain relevant in a world marked by change and how they can continue to enrich and strengthen marriages.

9.1 The Ever-Changing Landscape

The modern world is marked by rapid change and shifting cultural norms. This section explores the dynamics of modern relationships and how Christian marriage values can serve as a stabilizing force amidst these changes.

9.2 Navigating Gender Equality

In contemporary society, the concept of marriage is evolving, particularly with regard to gender roles and equality within partnerships. This chapter delves into how Christian values of cherishing and honoring can inform these shifting dynamics and promote mutual respect and collaboration.

9.3 Technology and Connection

The digital age has transformed the way we connect and communicate. This section examines the role of technology in modern marriages, both as a tool for connection and as a potential source of conflict, and how Christian values can guide couples in using technology mindfully.

## 9.4 Cherishing Love Amidst Distractions

Modern life is often marked by busy schedules and constant distractions. The chapter explores how Christian couples can prioritize cherishing and honoring amidst the demands of work, technology, and other obligations.

## 9.5 Multicultural and Interfaith Marriages

In today's globalized world, many marriages are multicultural or interfaith. This section examines the role of Christian values in promoting understanding, respect, and unity within these diverse partnerships.

## 9.6 Nurturing Faith in a Secular World

The modern world is often marked by secularism and skepticism. This chapter explores how Christian couples can nurture and strengthen their faith within a secular context, as well as how they can set an example for others seeking a meaningful spiritual connection in their lives.

## 9.7 The Power of Adaptation

In the face of these modern challenges, Christian marriage values remain powerful and adaptable. This chapter explores the resilience and flexibility of these values, highlighting their ability to guide couples through the complexities of contemporary life.

As we navigate through the final chapter, we explore the relevance and adaptability of Christian marriage values of cherishing and honoring in the modern world. This chapter serves as a guide for couples seeking to strengthen their relationships and live out these enduring values in a changing and dynamic society, emphasizing that faith, love, and commitment remain as essential as ever in the journey of marriage.

# 10

# A Testament of Faith

In this concluding chapter, "A Testament of Faith," we reflect on the enduring impact of Christian marriage values in the lives of Sarah and John, and in the lives of readers who have followed their journey. This chapter serves as a testimony to the transformative power of faith, love, and commitment within the sacred covenant of marriage.

10.1 A Lifelong Covenant

For Sarah and John, their marriage has been a sacred covenant that has endured the test of time. They have cherished and honored each other through the years, reflecting the deep commitment and unshakable faith that has been their guiding light.

10.2 A Family of Faith

Their commitment to Christian values has not only enriched their marriage but has also permeated their family life. The faith they've nurtured together has become a defining element of their family's identity and an enduring legacy for their children and future generations.

10.3 A Light to Others

Their marriage has served as a beacon of hope and inspiration for others, both within their faith community and beyond. As they've journeyed through life, their love, respect, and commitment to one another have touched the hearts of those around them, demonstrating the beauty of Christian marriage values in action.

10.4 A Living Example of Love

Through the challenges and joys they've faced, Sarah and John have shown that the power of love, when rooted in faith, can overcome adversity and flourish over time. Their story is a living example of the transformative effect of Christian values on marriage.

10.5 A Continuation of Tradition

Their marriage reflects the continuation of the tradition of cherishing and honoring in Christian matrimony. It stands as a testament to the enduring relevance of these values in the face of changing times, and as an invitation for others to embrace these principles in their own lives.

10.6 A Call to Action

The chapter concludes with a call to action for readers, urging them to reflect on their own relationships, the role of faith and values in their lives, and their commitment to cherishing and honoring their loved ones. It inspires individuals to seek the enduring and transformative power of faith, love, and commitment in their own journeys.

As we journey through this final chapter, we witness the lifelong impact of Christian marriage values on the lives of Sarah and John, as well as the broader community. Their marriage is a living testament to the enduring power of love, faith, and commitment in the sacred covenant of matrimony, offering inspiration, hope, and a profound sense of purpose to those who have followed their journey.

# 11

# Nurturing Love for Generations

In this chapter, "Nurturing Love for Generations," we explore how Christian marriage values continue to thrive in the lives of Sarah and John, their children, and their grandchildren. It offers a testament to the enduring legacy of faith, love, and commitment within the sacred covenant of Christian marriage.

11.1 Passing the Torch

Sarah and John's commitment to cherishing and honoring each other has a profound impact on the generations that follow. As they look at their children and grandchildren, they see the values they've nurtured being passed on to a new generation.

11.2 Cherish and Honor Through the Years

The enduring love between Sarah and John serves as an inspiration for their children and grandchildren. It demonstrates the beauty of love that deepens and matures over time, reminding them that love is not fleeting but can grow stronger with each passing year.

11.3 Strengthening the Family Bond

The commitment to Christian values has not only enriched Sarah and John's marriage but has also strengthened the bond within their family. Their home is a place of love, respect, and faith, providing a solid foundation for the generations that follow.

## 11.4 Cherish and Honor in Their Own Lives

Sarah and John's children and grandchildren, influenced by their example, apply the principles of cherishing and honoring in their own relationships. They carry the torch of love, respect, and faith into their own marriages, reflecting the enduring legacy of Christian values.

## 11.5 Cherishing Traditions

This chapter explores the traditions and customs that Sarah and John have established over the years, which serve as a living reminder of the values they've upheld. These traditions create a sense of continuity and reinforce the importance of cherishing and honoring in their family.

## 11.6 Celebrating Milestones

As the years pass, Sarah and John's family continue to celebrate milestones, from anniversaries to family gatherings. These moments provide an opportunity for reflection and gratitude, as well as an occasion to renew their commitment to Christian marriage values.

## 11.7 A Legacy of Love

Sarah and John's legacy is not just the values they've nurtured; it is the love they've passed down. Their commitment to faith, love, and cherishing one another has created a legacy of love that will continue to enrich the lives of their descendants for generations to come.

This chapter serves as a reflection on the enduring impact of Christian marriage values within the lives of Sarah and John and their extended family. Their story is a testament to the transformative power of faith, love, and commitment within the sacred covenant of marriage, offering inspiration, hope, and a profound sense of purpose to the generations they nurture and influence.

# 12

# A Love That Endures

In this final chapter, "A Love That Endures," we explore the evergreen qualities of Christian marriage values and their enduring significance in the lives of Sarah and John. This chapter is a reflection on the timeless nature of faith, love, and commitment in the sacred covenant of marriage.

12.1 Time-Tested Commitment

Sarah and John's journey has been a testament to the time-tested commitment inherent in Christian marriage values. Their enduring love and devotion to one another are a living example of how faith, love, and commitment can withstand the trials and tribulations of life.

12.2 The Ever-Deepening Bond

Their marriage reflects a love that deepens with time, and their commitment to cherishing and honoring each other has grown richer over the years. Their journey demonstrates that love, when rooted in faith, continues to flourish as it matures.

12.3 A Legacy of Faith

As Sarah and John have lived out their Christian marriage values, their faith has left an indelible mark on their family and community. Their unwavering commitment to their beliefs has created a legacy of faith that serves as a source of inspiration for others.

## 12.4 A Testament to Love

Their love story serves as a testament to the enduring power of love. It is a living example of how love can overcome adversity, deepen with age, and remain steadfast in the face of life's challenges.

## 12.5 A Hopeful Future

As they reflect on their journey, Sarah and John look to the future with hope. Their enduring love is not just a testament to their past but also a source of anticipation for the years to come.

## 12.6 A Call to Perpetuate Values

This chapter concludes with a call to perpetuate the values of faith, love, and commitment in the sacred covenant of marriage. It encourages readers to reflect on the enduring nature of these values and the profound impact they can have on their own lives.

As we journey through this final chapter, we witness the enduring impact of Christian marriage values on the lives of Sarah and John. Their story is a testament to the enduring power of faith, love, and commitment within the sacred covenant of matrimony, offering inspiration, hope, and a profound sense of purpose to those who seek to embrace these values in their own lives.

Book Summary: Cherish and Honor: Christian Marriage Values

"Cherish and Honor: Christian Marriage Values" is a heartfelt exploration of the enduring and transformative power of faith, love, and commitment within the sacred covenant of Christian marriage. Through the captivating story of Sarah and John, the book takes readers on a journey that spans generations, unveiling the profound significance of these values at every stage of life.

The book consists of twelve chapters, each focusing on a specific facet of Christian marriage values. It begins by introducing the central themes of cherishing and honoring, emphasizing their deep roots in Christian faith. As the narrative unfolds, readers witness the wedding of Sarah and John, where these values become the cornerstone of their journey.

Throughout the book, the biblical foundations of faith, love, and commitment are explored, highlighting the importance of these values as a reflection of Christ's love for His Church. The authors delve into the practical applications of these values in areas such as communication, conflict resolution, and the nurturing of love over time.

Readers witness the resilience and adaptability of Christian marriage values as Sarah and John navigate the modern world, where traditional norms are challenged by changing gender dynamics, technological advancements, and shifting cultural paradigms. The book underscores how these values remain relevant, serving as guiding principles in contemporary relationships and marriages.

As Sarah and John's journey progresses, the book showcases their enduring commitment to one another, offering a powerful testimony to the strength of faith, love, and honor as they overcome trials and celebrate milestones. The enduring impact of these values is felt not only within their marriage but also in the lives of their children and grandchildren.

The narrative concludes with a call to action, inviting readers to reflect on the enduring nature of these values and their potential to enrich their own lives and relationships. "Cherish and Honor: Christian Marriage Values" is a testament to the evergreen qualities of these values, offering inspiration, hope, and a profound sense of purpose to those who seek to embrace them within their own sacred covenants of marriage.

www.ingramcontent.com/pod-product-compliance
Lightning Source LLC
LaVergne TN
LVHW010440070526
838199LV00066B/6108